BY ALLAN MOREY

THE PITTSBURGH
STEELERS
STORY

BELLWETHER MEDIA · MINNEAPOLIS, MN

Are you ready to take it to the extreme? Torque books thrust you into the action-packed world of sports, vehicles, mystery, and adventure. These books may include dirt, smoke, fire, and chilling tales. **WARNING**: read at your own risk.

This edition first published in 2017 by Bellwether Media, Inc.

No part of this publication may be reproduced in whole or in part without written permission of the publisher. For information regarding permission, write to Bellwether Media, Inc., Attention: Permissions Department, 5357 Penn Avenue South, Minneapolis, MN 55419.

Library of Congress Cataloging-in-Publication Data

Names: Morey, Allan.
Title: The Pittsburgh Steelers Story / by Allan Morey.
Description: Minneapolis, MN : Bellwether Media, Inc., 2017. | Series:
  Torque: NFL Teams | Includes index. | Audience: Ages: 7-12.
Identifiers: LCCN 2015040041 | ISBN 9781626173798 (hardcover : alk. paper)
Subjects: LCSH: Pittsburgh Steelers (Football team)–History–Juvenile literature.
Classification: LCC GV956.P57 M67 2017 | DDC 796.332/640974886–dc23
LC record available at http://lccn.loc.gov/2015040041

Printed in the United States of America, North Mankato, MN.

TABLE OF CONTENTS

In **Super Bowl** 43, the Pittsburgh Steelers battle the Arizona Cardinals. The Steelers lead 10 to 7 late in the first half.

Ben Roethlisberger

SUPER BOWL RECORD
Harrison ran his interception back 100 yards. That is a Super Bowl record!

But the Cardinals are driving. They get down to the 1-yard line. Then Steelers linebacker James Harrison intercepts a pass. He runs the ball back for a touchdown!

Santonio Holmes

The Steelers push their lead 20 to 7. But then the Cardinals take over. After a safety and two touchdowns, they lead by 3 points.

With two minutes left, the Steelers have the ball. Quarterback Ben Roethlisberger marches his team down the field. He tosses a short pass to wide receiver Santonio Holmes. Touchdown! Steelers win!

SCORING TERMS

END ZONE

the area at each end of a football field; a team scores by entering the opponent's end zone with the football.

EXTRA POINT

a score that occurs when a kicker kicks the ball between the opponent's goal posts after a touchdown is scored; 1 point.

FIELD GOAL

a score that occurs when a kicker kicks the ball between the opponent's goal posts; 3 points.

SAFETY

a score that occurs when a player on offense is tackled behind his own goal line; 2 points for defense.

TOUCHDOWN

a score that occurs when a team crosses into its opponent's end zone with the football; 6 points.

TWO-POINT CONVERSION

a score that occurs when a team crosses into its opponent's end zone with the football after scoring a touchdown; 2 points.

The Steelers have always been known for their **defense**. In the 1970s, their **defensive linemen** were called the "Steel Curtain." They led the charge as Pittsburgh won four Super Bowls in six years.

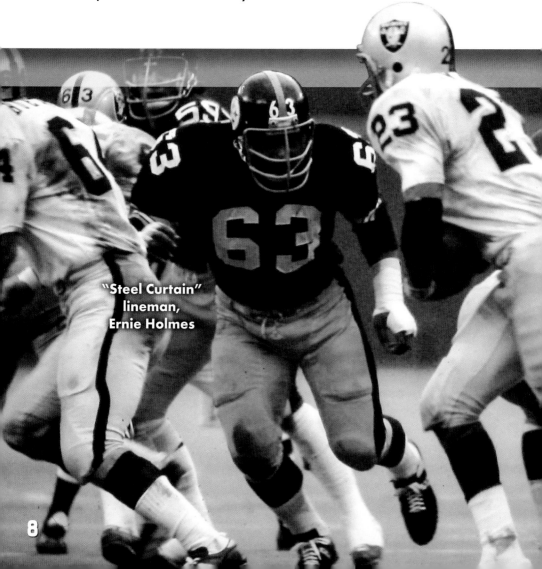

"Steel Curtain" lineman, Ernie Holmes

The Steelers have held
on to that tradition. A tough
defense helped them win
two more Super Bowls in
the 2000s.

The Steelers started out as the Pirates. But the team was renamed for Pittsburgh's booming steel industry. One of Pittsburgh's nicknames is the "Steel City."

Since 2001, the Steelers have played at Heinz Field. The stadium sits along the Ohio River. It is named for the city's famous ketchup company.

GIANT KETCHUP BOTTLES
Two giant neon ketchup bottles are part of Heinz Field's scoreboard.

HEINZ FIELD

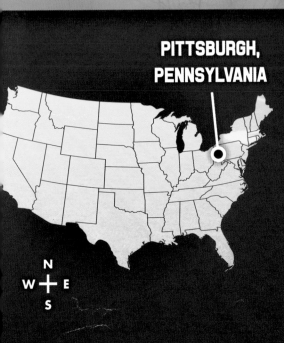

PITTSBURGH,
PENNSYLVANIA

N
W + E
S

11

The Steelers joined the National Football League (NFL) in 1933. They play in the American Football Conference (AFC). They are in the North Division.

The North Division has the Baltimore Ravens, Cleveland Browns, and Cincinnati Bengals. Many fans call the Ravens the Steelers' biggest rival. Their games are known for being hard-hitting.

NFL DIVISIONS

AFC

AFC NORTH

BALTIMORE RAVENS

CINCINNATI BENGALS

CLEVELAND BROWNS

PITTSBURGH STEELERS

AFC EAST

BUFFALO BILLS

MIAMI DOLPHINS

NEW ENGLAND PATRIOTS

NEW YORK JETS

AFC SOUTH

HOUSTON TEXANS

INDIANAPOLIS COLTS

JACKSONVILLE JAGUARS

TENNESSEE TITANS

AFC WEST

DENVER BRONCOS

KANSAS CITY CHIEFS

OAKLAND RAIDERS

SAN DIEGO CHARGERS

THE STEAGLES

In 1943, the Steelers and Philadelphia Eagles joined teams because of World War II. They were called the Steagles that year.

NFC

NFC NORTH

CHICAGO
BEARS

DETROIT
LIONS

GREEN BAY
PACKERS

MINNESOTA
VIKINGS

NFC EAST

DALLAS
COWBOYS

NEW YORK
GIANTS

PHILADELPHIA
EAGLES

WASHINGTON
REDSKINS

NFC SOUTH

ATLANTA
FALCONS

CAROLINA
PANTHERS

NEW ORLEANS
SAINTS

TAMPA BAY
BUCCANEERS

NFC WEST

ARIZONA
CARDINALS

LOS ANGELES
RAMS

SAN FRANCISCO
49ERS

SEATTLE
SEAHAWKS

The Steelers were not very good at first. From 1933 to 1971, the team had only seven winning seasons.

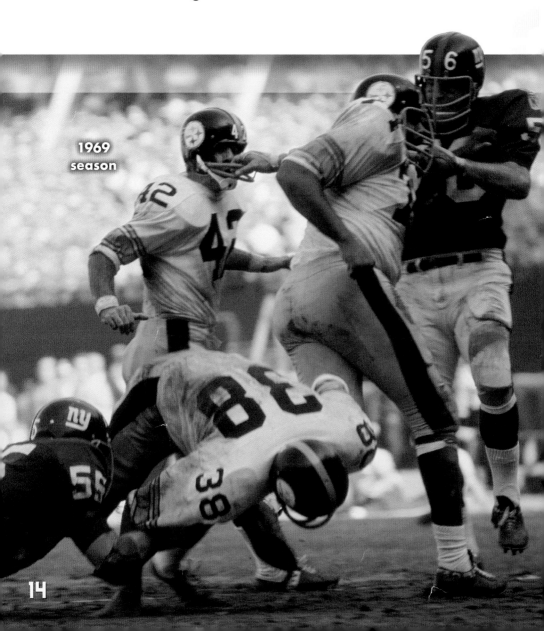

1969 season

Chuck Noll

Terry Bradshaw

Then head coach Chuck Noll turned things around. He built a crushing defense. He also **drafted** star quarterback Terry Bradshaw. From 1974 to 1979, the Steelers won four Super Bowls!

Bill Cowher

In 1992, Bill Cowher replaced Noll as coach. He led the team to many division titles and a fifth Super Bowl win.

Mike Tomlin became coach after Cowher. He took the Steelers to Super Bowl 43. The Steelers won and became the first team to win six Super Bowls!

Mike Tomlin

STEELERS
TIMELINE

1933

Joined the NFL as the Pittsburgh Pirates

1969

Hired head coach Chuck Noll

1975

Won Super Bowl 9, beating the Minnesota Vikings

16

FINAL SCORE

6

1940

Changed team name to the Pittsburgh Steelers

◄10 ◄20

1970

Drafted Hall-of-Fame quarterback Terry Bradshaw

1976

Won Super Bowl 10, beating the Dallas Cowboys

21 FINAL SCORE **17**

2004

Drafted quarterback Ben Roethlisberger

1979

Won Super Bowl 13, beating the Dallas Cowboys

35 FINAL SCORE **31**

2006

Won Super Bowl 40, beating the Seattle Seahawks

21 FINAL SCORE **10**

1980

Won Super Bowl 14, beating the Los Angeles Rams

31 FINAL SCORE **19**

2009

Won Super Bowl 43, beating the Arizona Cardinals

27 FINAL SCORE **23**

In the 1970s, four tough defensive linemen made up the Steel Curtain. They were led by "Mean" Joe Greene. He was one of the NFL's strongest defenders.

Joe Greene

Terry
Bradshaw

Lynn
Swann

Terry Bradshaw commanded the offense in the 1970s. His favorite target was wide receiver Lynn Swann. They played together in four Super Bowls.

Today, the Steelers are loaded with offensive talent. Quarterback Ben Roethlisberger has been the team's leader since 2004. He has played in three Super Bowls.

Roethlisberger's strong supporting cast includes Antonio Brown. He is one of the NFL's hardest-to-cover wide receivers.

TEAM GREATS

JOE GREENE
DEFENSIVE LINEMAN
1969-1981

TERRY BRADSHAW
QUARTERBACK
1970-1983

FRANCO HARRIS
RUNNING BACK
1972-1983

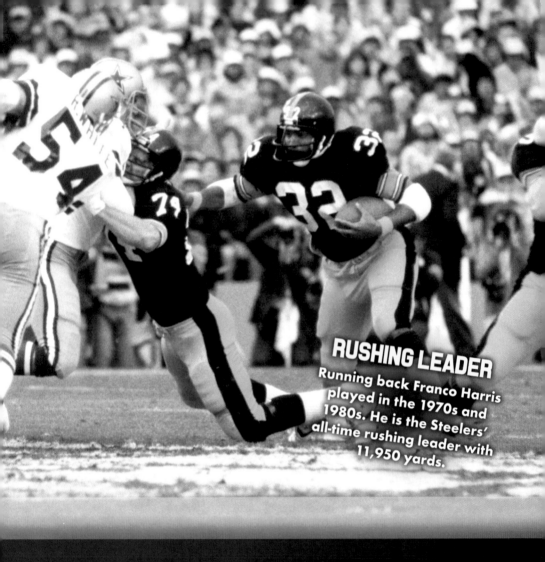

RUSHING LEADER

Running back Franco Harris played in the 1970s and 1980s. He is the Steelers' all-time rushing leader with 11,950 yards.

LYNN SWANN
WIDE RECEIVER
1974-1982

BEN ROETHLISBERGER
QUARTERBACK
2004-PRESENT

ANTONIO BROWN
WIDE RECEIVER
2010-PRESENT

The Steelers have a loyal following. Fans pack sold-out Heinz Field on game days.

Since the 1970s, the Steelers' winning ways have earned them many fans. People around the country and the world cheer them on. Their fans are known as "Steeler Nation."

SELLOUT STREAK

The Steelers have one of the NFL's longest sellout streaks. Their home games have been sold out since late in the 1972 season.

Fans proudly wave bright yellow "Terrible Towels" at games. These rally towels have become a symbol of the Steelers and the city of Pittsburgh itself.

Fans take their towels all over the world and beyond. Some have wrapped babies in Pittsburgh hospitals. One towel went all the way to the International Space Station!

COPE'S CREATION

Radio announcer Myron Cope came up with the Terrible Towel. He wanted fans to have something they could carry with them to show support for the team.

MORE ABOUT THE
STEELERS

Team name:
Pittsburgh Steelers

Team name explained:
**Named for Pittsburgh's
steel industry**

**Nicknames: The Black
and Gold, Men of Steel**

Joined NFL: 1933

Conference: AFC

Division: North

**Main rivals: Baltimore Ravens,
Cincinnati Bengals**

PENNSYLVANIA

PITTSBURGH

N
W + E
S

Home stadium name: **Heinz Field**

Stadium opened: **2001**

Seats in stadium: **68,400**

Logo: **A white circle outlined in gray, with yellow, red, and blue diamond shapes; colors represent the materials used for making steel: yellow for coal, red for iron ore, and blue for scrap steel.**

Colors: **Black, gold, white**

Steelers

Name for fan base: **Steeler Nation**

Mascot: **Steely McBeam**

GLOSSARY

conference—a large grouping of sports teams that often play one another

defense—the group of players who try to stop opposing teams from scoring

defensive linemen—players on defense whose main job is to try to stop the quarterback; defensive linemen crouch down in front of the ball.

division—a small grouping of sports teams that often play one another; usually there are several divisions of teams in a conference.

drafted—chose a college athlete to play for a professional team

intercepts—catches a pass thrown by the opposing team

linebacker—a player on defense whose main job is to make tackles and stop passes; a linebacker stands just behind the defensive linemen.

offense—the group of players who try to move down the field and score

quarterback—a player on offense whose main job is to throw and hand off the ball

rival—a long-standing opponent

Super Bowl—the championship game for the NFL

wide receiver—a player on offense whose main job is to catch passes from the quarterback

TO LEARN MORE

AT THE LIBRARY

Anastasio, Dina. *What Is the Super Bowl?* New York, N.Y.: Grosset & Dunlap, 2015.

Burgess, Zack. *Meet the Pittsburgh Steelers.* Chicago, Ill.: Norwood House Press, 2016.

Frisch, Aaron. *Pittsburgh Steelers.* Mankato, Minn.: Creative Education, 2014.

ON THE WEB

Learning more about the Pittsburgh Steelers is as easy as 1, 2, 3.

1. Go to www.factsurfer.com.

2. Enter "Pittsburgh Steelers" into the search box.

3. Click the "Surf" button and you will see a list of related web sites.

With factsurfer.com, finding more information is just a click away.

INDEX